C000135219

SHADES of SOUND
Winter

A LISTENING & COLORING BOOK FOR PIANISTS

by
Jennifer Boster, NCTM

A Listening & Coloring Book for Pianists

By Jennifer Boster, NCTM

Copyright ©2019 Jennifer Boster
The Playful Piano | theplayfulpiano.com

All rights reserved. No part of this publication may be reproduced or transmitted in any form or by any means without permission.

The Playful Piano
PO Box 12931
Ogden, UT 84412-2931
USA

Introduction

My goal in creating the Shades of Sound listening curriculum is to help piano students gain an interest in and a love and appreciation for great classical music.

Aspiring pianists need to know the literature, hear the greats perform, and be inspired and excited by the great music that is available! Just as writers need to read, read, read, pianists need to listen! Through this fun curriculum, students will learn about the great composers and their works. Listening repertoire selected includes selections from the solo piano literature, as well as piano and orchestra literature, and orchestral works.

My hope is that students can add just 5-10 minutes of listening per day to their normal practicing. Listening to great music will change their understanding of music and will vastly increase their music history knowledge. It will excite and inspire them, encourage further study and listening, give them new pieces to add to their own repertoire wish list, infuse more great music into their lives, homes and families, and will boost their musicianship and expression to the next level.

Winter

This volume of the series focuses on music for the winter season. Half of the music in this collection is for solo piano, while the other half draws upon the rich musical literature for orchestra, choir and chamber music. This collection of music is full of wintery ambience, whether it be bleak and desolate or sparkling and spirited. Musical periods represented include Baroque, Romantic, Impressionist and Contemporary. Visit a musical world of snowstorms, ice skating, Arctic glaciers, sleigh rides and winter wind. I hope you enjoy this book!

How to Use This Book

Read

First read the background information about the piece. Each piece featured in this book includes the following information: piece title, composer name and dates, and interesting background information on that particular piece. There is also a section called "What to listen for" and a question or two to help encourage active listening and learning. I have also included the approximate time of each piece (according to the recordings I selected for the playlist).

Listen

Search for and pull up **"The Playful Piano - Shades of Sound: Winter"** playlist on YouTube (or scan this handy QR code!). All selections included in this book are in that list in the same order they appear here. I have chosen videos for each selection that are of good quality and will be inspirational and educational.

As you listen, rate each piece by coloring in the stars. Five stars means "I loved this piece so much!" and one star means "I didn't really care for this piece." My hope is that students will find things to learn and appreciate about each selection, whether it becomes a favorite piece or not.

Color

As you listen to each piece, have fun coloring the accompanying coloring page! Jot down any notes or thoughts and answer the questions on the previous page.

Create a Repertoire Wish List

The "Repertoire Wish List" is a place for students to record pieces that they absolutely love and would love to learn someday! I hope that students will get excited about the rich variety of piano repertoire available and be inspired to learn some of the pieces they hear.

Happy Listening!

—Jennifer Boster

ThePlayfulPiano.com

Repertoire Wish List

Pieces I have heard and would LOVE to learn!

Piece Title	Composer

The Snow is Dancing

Piece: **Children's Corner, L. 113: IV. The Snow is Dancing**

Composer: **Claude Debussy**, 1862-1918, France

2 ½ minutes

About the composer: Claude Debussy was a French composer who is generally known as the first Impressionist composer. He was a very influential figure in twentieth-century music. His pianistic style was characterized by layers of sound and color, lots of unresolved harmonies and parallel chords.

About the piece: Debussy dedicated the *Children's Corner Suite* to his three-year-old daughter, Chou-Chou. It was published in 1908 and includes six pieces that are reminiscent of childhood. Hinson calls it an "exquisite set" that is similar to Schumann's *Kinderscenen*. *The Snow is Dancing* is the fourth movement of the set.

What to listen for: The piece begins with a simple pattern of four rising stepwise notes beginning on E. This pattern continues through much of the piece; through this repeated pattern and also through the alternating of notes between hands, Debussy created the mesmerizing sound of snow swirling and whirling.

Try playing this pattern of notes on the piano, and then as you listen to the piece see if you can hear that pattern recurring throughout the music.

Debussy – The Snow is Dancing

Rate this piece: ⭐☆☆☆☆

What I like about this piece:	How I would describe this piece:

Footsteps in the Snow

Piece: **Preludes - Book 1: 6. Des Pas Sur la Neige**

Composer: **Claude Debussy**, 1862-1918, France

5 minutes

About the piece: This piece is one of Debussy's beautiful twenty-four Preludes. These short, impressionistic pieces have highly descriptive titles which were written at the end of each piece, allowing one to experience the music first before being influenced by the composer's intended subject.

What to listen for: Debussy masterfully composed this simple prelude based on two tiny motives, - D to E, then E to F - as if they are two footsteps, left foot then right foot, in the frozen snow.

Try playing the simple motive on the next page on the piano before listening, so you can recognize the musical footsteps as you hear them in the music. Listen to this piece with your eyes closed. Can you picture in your mind the white snowy landscape? What does your wintry scene look like to you?

Rate this piece: ☆☆☆☆☆

What I like about this piece:	How I would describe this piece:

Winter Wind

Piece: **12 Etudes, Op. 25: No. 11 in A Minor, "Winter Wind"**
Composer: **Frederic Chopin**, 1810-1849, Poland

4 minutes

About the composer: Frederic Chopin, the Polish pianist and composer, was one of the greatest composers for the piano of all time. A child prodigy, he moved to Paris at the age of twenty-one where he composed, taught piano and sometimes performed. His piano compositions are highly original and full of "faultless grace" (Hinson). His works should be central to the education of any pianist.

About the piece: In the early nineteenth century there was a widespread fascination with virtuosity, leading to the popularity of the *etude* – a composition designed to improve the technique and virtuosity of the performer. Chopin's twenty-seven etudes were not only meant for technique study but also for public performance. His "Winter Wind" etude is considered one of the most difficult of all of the etudes. Huneker said this about this etude: "It takes prodigious power and endurance to play this work, prodigious power, passion and no little poetry… Small souled men, no matter how agile their fingers, should avoid it."

What to listen for: Listen for a relentless cascade of tumultuous sixteenth notes in the right hand, testing the stamina and dexterity of the performer.

Rate this piece: ☆ ☆ ☆ ☆ ☆

What I like about this piece:	How I would describe this piece:

The Four Seasons: Winter

Piece: **The Four Seasons, Concerto No. 4 in F Minor, RV 297 "Winter"**

Composer: **Antonio Vivaldi**, 1678-1741, Italy

9 minutes

About the composer: Antonio Vivaldi was an Italian violinist and composer of the late baroque period known especially for his instrumental music, including over five hundred concertos.

About the piece: Written in 1720, *The Four Seasons* is Vivaldi's most famous work. It is a set of four violin concertos, each based on one of the four seasons of the year. Each concerto is comprised of three movements, and Vivaldi published each movement with a poem. The poems published with "Winter" are as follows:

Allegro non molto
Frozen and shivering in the icy snow,
In the severe blasts of a terrible wind
To run stamping one's feet each moment,
One's teeth chattering through the cold.

Largo
To spend quiet and happy times by the fire
While outside the rain soaks everyone.

Allegro
To walk on the ice with tentative steps,
Going carefully for fear of falling.

To go in haste, slide, and fall down to the ground,
To go again on the ice and run,
In case the ice cracks and opens.

To hear leaving their iron-gated house Sirocco,
Boreas, and all the winds in battle—
This is winter, but it brings joy.

Vivaldi – The Four Seasons: Winter

What to listen for: Read the poem that goes with each movement, and then listen for moments in the music that relate to the poetry – chattering teeth represented by the violin section, a warm violin melody accompanied by plucked violin raindrops, and tentative steps on slippery ice created by long legato phrases.

Rate this piece: ☆ ☆ ☆ ☆ ☆

What I like about this piece:	How I would describe this piece:

Recomposed: Winter

Piece: **Recomposed: Vivaldi, The Four Seasons: Winter**

Composer: **Max Richter**, born 1966, Germany

11 minutes

About the composer: Max Richter is a contemporary Classical composer whose works include award-winning film scores, chart-topping Classical albums, solo instrumental works and collaborations with other artists.

About the piece: For this piece, Richter put his own spin on Vivaldi's "Winter" from *The Four Seasons*. He gave it a contemporary flair while still remaining true to Vivaldi's masterpiece. After it was released, *Recomposed: The Four Seasons* topped the Classical music charts in 22 countries. Like Vivaldi's version, Richter's is comprised of three movements; his are entitled *Winter 1*, *Winter 2* and *Winter 3*.

What to listen for: Richter says this about *Winter 3*: *"I'm happy with the way Winter 3 turned out - the sense of falling that this music has and the way that you can listen into the texture. There is deliberately more going on in the music than we can hear at any one time: the searching solo line, the various descending upper orchestral string lines, the lower chorale-like material - we cannot take it in as a whole, but, like a landscape, we can explore it bit by bit, listening in to its various surfaces. I personally enjoy music that allows that sort of interaction."*

Rate this piece: ⭐⭐⭐⭐⭐

What I like about this piece:	How I would describe this piece:

Improvisation on Winter

Piece: Improvisation on Vivaldi: Winter – The Four Seasons

Composer: **Gabriela Montero**, born 1970, Venezuela

5 minutes

About the composer: Gabriela Montero is a Venezuelan concert pianist, composer and improviser. Her first public performance was at the age of five, and her first concerto performance with an orchestra was at age eight. She has performed with many of the world's most-respected orchestras. Montero is celebrated not only for her brilliant and visionary interpretations, but for her ability to improvise and compose pieces in real-time. She has written other works, including a tone poem for piano and orchestra and a piano concerto.

About the piece: This beautiful improvisation is based on the second movement of Vivaldi's *Winter*.

What to listen for: Can you hear the theme from Vivaldi's *Winter*? Listen as she effortlessly improvises a gorgeous arrangement of this theme.

Rate this piece: ☆ ☆ ☆ ☆ ☆

What I like about this piece:

How I would describe this piece:

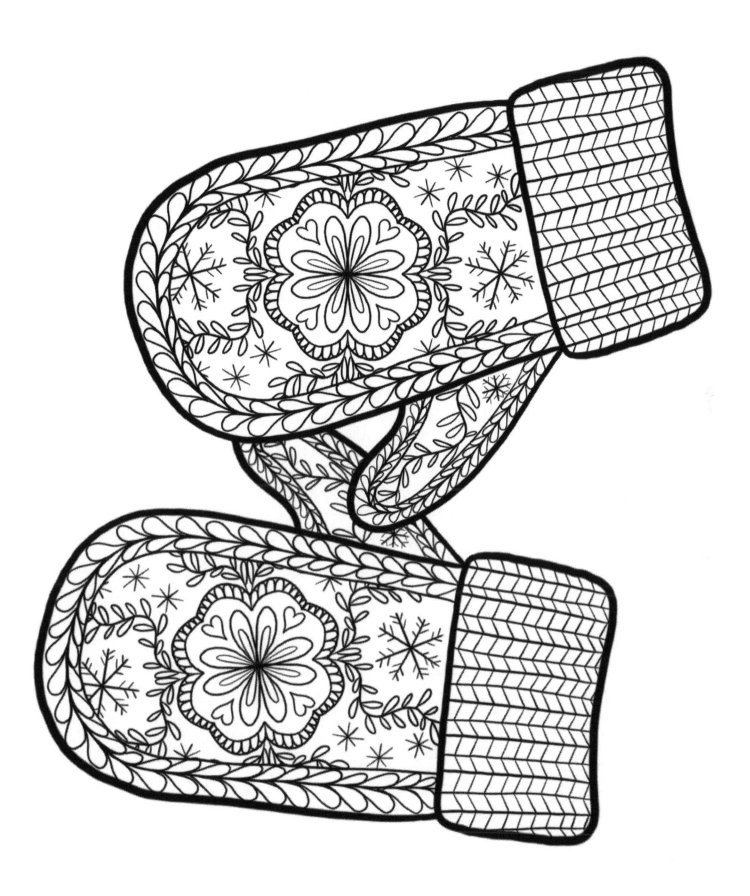

Winter Fairy

Piece: **10 Pieces from Cinderella, Op. 97: No. 4, Winter Fairy**

Composer: **Sergei Prokofiev**, 1891-1953, Russia

3 ½ minutes

About the composer: Sergei Prokofiev was an important Russian composer and pianist with a very individual style. His works had percussive elements, lyricism, energetic rhythms and strong dissonant harmonies. He was greatly influenced by Russian folk songs.

About the piece: In the 1940's, Prokofiev composed music for the ballet *Cinderella*. Although this was an orchestral score, he also transcribed much of the music for solo piano and released it before the ballet was first performed. Included in the opus 97 set of ten pieces is a short character piece for the fairies of each season, who help get Cinderella ready for the ball. In this piece, the Winter Fairy is magically changing ice into a diamond crown and a sparkling cloak for Cinderella.

What to listen for: Hear notes rising and falling over and over as the fairy slowly flitters through the cold air.

Rate this piece: ☆☆☆☆☆

What I like about this piece:	How I would describe this piece:

Troika

Piece: **Lieutenant Kije. Symphonic Suite, Op. 60: IV. Troika. Moderato – Allegro con brio**

Composer: **Sergei Prokofiev**, 1891-1953, Russia

3 minutes

About the piece: Prokofiev's *Lieutenant Kije* was originally written as a film score for a film of the same name. The suite has become one of his most well-known works. This piece depicts a Russian *troika* - a type of Russian sleigh pulled by three horses.

What to listen for: This exciting piece for orchestra is full of warmth and movement. Hear the sleigh bells jingle as the sleigh speeds across the frozen ground. As the woodwinds play the theme the strings begin to add a whirling counterpoint theme of their own – can you hear the snow flurries swirling around the moving sleigh?

Rate this piece: ★ ☆ ☆ ☆ ☆

What I like about this piece:	How I would describe this piece:

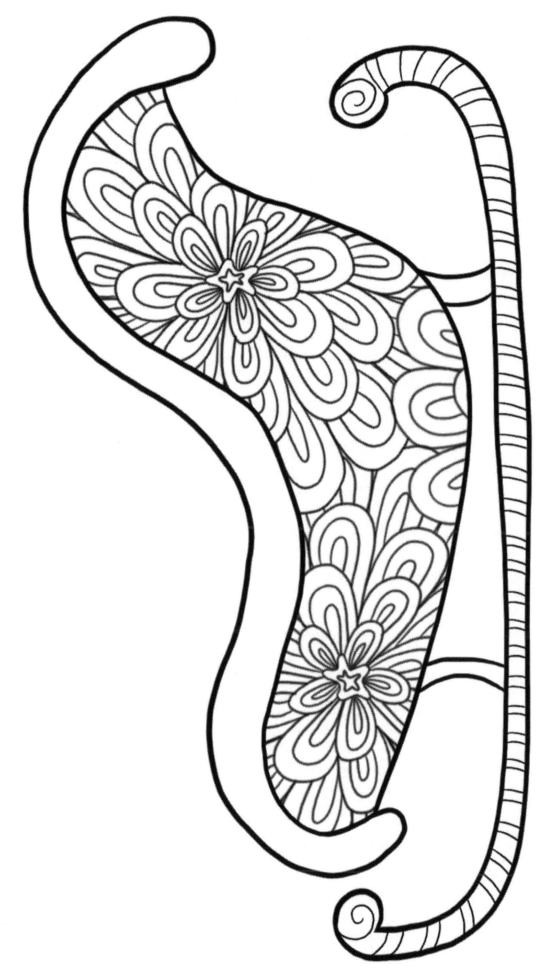

The Skaters' Waltz

Piece: **Les patineurs ("The Skater's Waltz"), Op. 183**

Composer: **Emile Waldteufel,** 1837-1915, France

7 ½ minutes

About the composer: Emile Waldteufel was a French pianist, composer and conductor who came from a family of musicians – his father and brother were both violinists and composers. Waldteufel studied at the Paris Conservatory. Most of his compositions were waltzes.

About the piece: The Skater's Waltz is Waldteufel's most famous composition. It has been featured in many films and other media throughout the years – for example, Rabbit hums it while ice skating in *The Many Adventures of Winnie the Pooh*; it is also quoted in Ernest Tomlinson's *Fantasia on Auld Lang Syne*. This piece depicts a wintry day in Paris.

What to listen for: This waltz begins with the horn playing the opening theme slowly. The strings then take over, repeating the main theme in a more lively waltz tempo. It then alternates back and forth between contrasting sections, with different instrument sections taking the lead at different times. Listen for sleigh bells and for lots of glittering wintry ambience.

Rate this piece: ☆☆☆☆☆

What I like about this piece:	How I would describe this piece:

Prelude & Fugue in C minor

Piece: **The Well-Tempered Clavier, Book I: Prelude & Fugue No. 2 in C minor, BWV 847**

Composer: **Johann Sebastian Bach**, 1685-1750, Germany

3 minutes

About the composer: Johann Sebastian Bach is one of the greatest and most famous composers of all time, and one of the greatest geniuses in the history of music. He lived in Germany and came from a family of musicians. Some of his most famous works are his *Well-Tempered Clavier* and his *Brandenburg Concertos*.

About the piece: This is the second prelude and fugue in Bach's *Well-Tempered Clavier*, a collection for which he composed a prelude and fugue in each of the twenty-four major and minor keys.

What to listen for: The prelude consists of contrasting sections – a rapid, presto section (perhaps reminiscent of a winter blizzard?) followed by a slower, free section that ends and resolves the piece. This toccata-like piece requires good technique and dexterity. The fugue is written in three voices, so listen for three distinct parts, each repeating the same theme and thematic material.

Rate this piece: ☆☆☆☆☆

What I like about this piece:	How I would describe this piece:

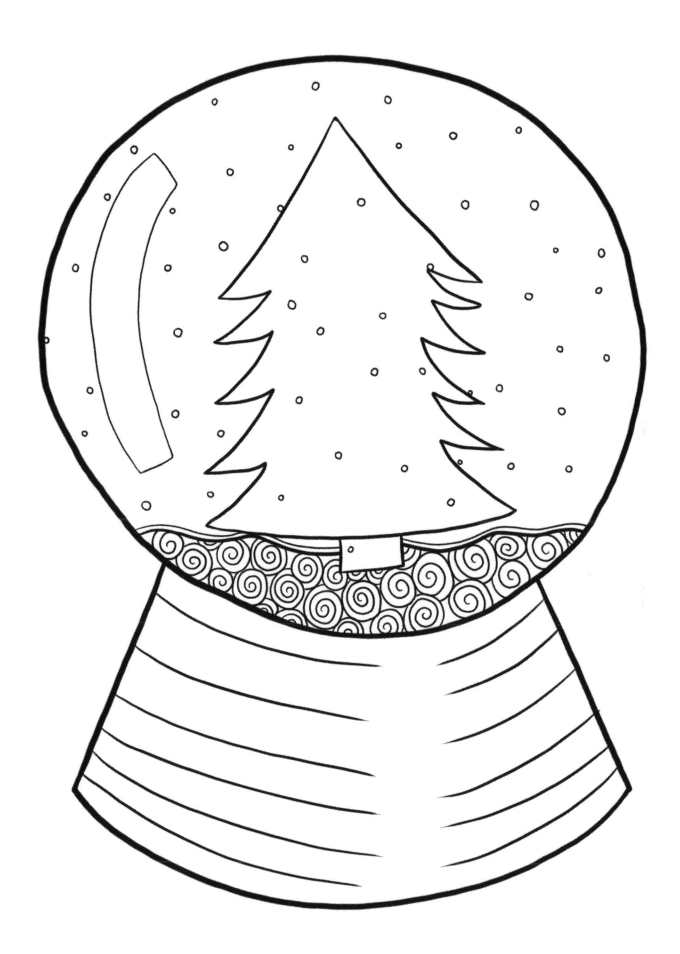

Passaggio

Piece: **Passaggio**

Composer: **Ludovico Einaudi**, born 1955, Italy

5 minutes

About the composer: Ludovico Einaudi is a classically-trained Italian composer and pianist who enjoys wide-spread popularity for his music. His works use a blend of elements including classical, electronic, rock and world music. He has topped both classical and pop music charts, sold out prestigious concert halls around the world and won awards for film scores. He enjoys bringing his music to a large audience through the internet and social media.

About the piece: This piece was originally written for solo piano, but here we hear it arranged for piano and violin. The Italian word *passaggio* means "passage;" in music it can refer to the transition between vocal registers for singers, or an improvised embellishment in sixteenth-century music. This piece originally came from Einaudi's album *Le Onde* which is based on the novel *The Waves* by Virginia Woolf.

What to listen for: This piece includes beautiful and haunting harmonies played in the piano while the violin plays a beautiful theme that is repeated later in a higher register.

Rate this piece: ☆☆☆☆☆

What I like about this piece:	How I would describe this piece:

Elegy for the Arctic

Piece: **Elegy for the Arctic**

Composer: **Ludovico Einaudi**, born 1955, Italy

3 ½ minutes

About the piece: This beautiful piece, composed in a minimalist style (a form of contemporary art music that uses limited musical materials), was actually premiered on a grand piano floating on a manmade "iceberg" near a crumbling glacier in Norway. The video was made to increase awareness of a campaign to help save the Arctic.

What to listen for: Listen for characteristics of minimalist music in this piece – consonant harmonies (or in traditional harmony, as opposed to dissonant), steady pulse and often-repeated themes and motifs.

Rate this piece: ⭐☆☆☆☆

What I like about this piece:	How I would describe this piece:

Stopping by Woods on a Snowy Evening

Piece: Frostiana: Seven Country Songs – Stopping by Woods on a Snowy Evening

Composer: Randall Thompson, 1899-1984, United States

6 minutes

About the composer: Randall Thompson was an American composer and teacher who enjoyed great popularity in the United States, particularly for his choral music. He wrote in a conservative and Neoclassical style, combining traditional and 20th-century styles.

About the piece: *Frostiana: Seven Country Songs* was commissioned by the town of Amherst, Massachusetts in 1959 for their bicentennial celebration. Robert Frost had taught at a local college there for many years and was friends with and admired the music of Randall Thompson. Thompson used the text of seven poems by Robert Frost in this seven-movement work for mixed chorus. This movement uses the text from one of Frost's most-loved and revered poems, "Stopping by Woods on a Snowy Evening:"

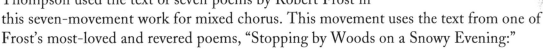

Whose woods these are I think I know.
His house is in the village though;
He will not see me stopping here
To watch his woods fill up with snow.

My little horse must think it queer
To stop without a farmhouse near
Between the woods and frozen lake
The darkest evening of the year.

He gives his harness bells a shake
To ask if there is some mistake.
The only other sound's the sweep
Of easy wind and downy flake.

The woods are lovely, dark and deep,
But I have promises to keep,
And miles to go before I sleep,
And miles to go before I sleep.

Thompson – Stopping by Woods on a Snowy Evening

What to listen for: In this beautiful song full of winter atmosphere, listen as the harp creates the sound of snow softly falling.

Rate this piece: ☆ ☆ ☆ ☆ ☆

What I like about this piece:	How I would describe this piece:

Before Spring

Piece: **Before Spring for Violin and Piano**

Composer: **Emma Lou Diemer**, born 1927, United States

11 minutes

About the composer: Emma Lou Diemer is an American composer, teacher and organist. A child prodigy, by the age of thirteen she had composed several piano concertos and was a church organist. She studied composition with famous contemporary composer Paul Hindemith. She is best-known for her works in the Neoclassical and Neoromantic styles, but her works encompass many styles, including twelve-tone serialism and extended techniques for organ and piano.

About the piece: This piece was written for piano and violin and was composed in 1997, near the end of the winter season. The composer says, "Even in Southern California spring seems to take a long time in coming…some of the suspense and anticipation of the full flowering of the seasons may be reflected in this work for violin and piano."

What to listen for: In composing this piece, Diemer played around with ideas and colors of the two instruments. Listen as the violin and piano begin by playing different notes and tonalities from each other. These musical ideas are weaved together, growing in intensity, becoming more lyrical at times and more agitated at others, then becoming calmer as the end grows near.

Rate this piece: ★ ☆ ☆ ☆ ☆

What I like about this piece:	How I would describe this piece:

Bibliography

Classic FM. "How I Wrote… Vivaldi's Four Seasons Recomposed – Max Richter." Classicfm.com. https://www.classicfm.com/composers/richter/news/vivaldi-recomposed-interview/ (Accessed February 6, 2019).

Editors of Encyclopedia Britannica. "Randall Thompson: American Composer." Britannica.com. https://www.britannica.com/biography/Randall-Thompson (Accessed February 5, 2019).

Emma Lou Diemer Music. "Emma Lou Diemer: Biography." Emmaloudiemermusic.com. http://www.emmaloudiemermusic.com/page/page/6385944.htm (Accessed February 5, 2019).

Gabriela Montero. "Gabriela Montero: Biography." Gabrielamontero.com. https://www.gabrielamontero.com/biography (Accessed February 6, 2019).

Gordon, Stewart. *A History of Keyboard Literature: Music for the Piano and its Forerunners.* Belmont, California: Wadsworth Group/Thomson Learning, 1996.

Hinson, Maurice, and Wesley Roberts. *Guide to the Pianist's Repertoire*, Fourth Edition, Kindle Edition. Bloomington: Indiana University Press, 2014.

Huneker, James. *Chopin: The Man and His Music.* Dover Publications, 1966.

Ludovico Einaudi. "Ludovico Einaudi: Bio." Ludovicoeinaudi.com. http://www.ludovicoeinaudi.com/en/bio.asp (Accessed February 5, 2019).

Max Richter Music. "Max Richter: Bio." Maxrichtermusic.com. https://www.maxrichtermusic.com/bio/ (Accessed February 6, 2019).

Naylor, Kirk. "Thompson's Frostiana: Seven Country Songs." MidAmerica Productions. http://midamerica-music.com/blog/thompsons-frostiana-seven-country-songs/ (Accessed February 5, 2019).

Randel, Don Michael, ed. *The Harvard Concise Dictionary of Music and Musicians.* Cambridge, Massachusetts: The Belknap Press of Harvard University Press, 1999.

Sadie, Julie Anne and Rhian Samuel, ed. *The Norton/Grove Dictionary of Women Composers.* New York, New York: W. W. Norton & Company, 1995.

Schlegel, Ellen Grolman. *Emma Lou Diemer: A Bio-bibliography.* Greenwood Publishing Group, 2001.

Schwarm, Betsy. "The Four Seasons by Vivaldi." Britannica.com. https://www.britannica.com/topic/The-Four-Seasons-by-Vivaldi (Accessed February 6, 2019).

Schwarm, Betsy. "The Skater's Waltz, Op. 183." Britannica.com. https://www.britannica.com/topic/The-Skaters-Waltz (Accessed February 7, 2019.)

Did you enjoy this book?
Please help me get the word out by
leaving me an Amazon review!

Check out the other Shades of Sound
Listening & Coloring Books in the series!

Shades of Sound: Women Composers
Shades of Sound: Halloween
Shades of Sound: Christmas
Shades of Sound: Valentine's Day
More titles coming soon!

the **PLAYFUL** piano

encouraging joyful music-making

preschool piano camps,
colorful technique booklets,
piano practicing resources
and more!

www.theplayfulpiano.com

Discover More Great Piano Teaching Resources at

theplayfulpiano.com

Save 10% at theplayfulpiano.com with coupon code

WINTER10

About the Author

Jenny Boster has been playing the piano and drawing ever since she was a little girl. She loves combining her interests to create fun and original resources for piano teachers. She has loved teaching piano lessons for twenty years! Jenny has a Bachelor of Music degree in Piano Performance from Brigham Young University and is a Nationally-Certified Teacher of Music. Jenny is passionate about encouraging students to listen to and gain a love for classical music. Her greatest joys are her husband, Jonathan, and being a mother to her five children.